Ha! Ha! Among the Trumpets by Alun Lewis

Alun Lewis was born on 1st July 1915 at Cwmaman, near Aberdare in the Cynon Valley in the South Wales Coalfield.

His parents were both school teachers at Ilanwern. Lewis was one of four children; a younger sister, and two brothers.

He was enthusiastic about writing from an early age. Lewis won a scholarship to attend Cowbridge Grammar School and from there went on to the University College of Wales and obtained a first in history in 1935. From there he went to the University of Manchester on a Pickles Research Fellowship and obtained his M.A in 1937.

Lewis first tried his hand at journalism but when he didn't succeed he turned to work as a supply teacher.

In 1939, Lewis met Gweno Ellis, a teacher, whom he later married on 5th July 1941.

Lewis was committed to pacifism but with the outbreak of World War II these principles were overcome by his desire to confront and defeat the evils of fascism. Enlisting, in 1940, he joined the Royal Engineers but then for reasons unknown he sought and gained a commission in an infantry battalion.

In 1941 he collaborated with artists John Petts and Brenda Chamberlain on the 'Caseg broadsheets'. These were inspired by chapbooks and broadside ballads and featured original woodcut artwork by Petts and poetry from prominent Welsh poets of the time including Dylan Thomas. Lewis was keen to create affordable literature for the masses. Unfortunately, sales were few and funds soon ran out.

His first published book, in 1942, was the poetry collection 'Raider's Dawn and Other Poems'. The same year a collection of short stories, 'The Last Inspection' followed. To round out the year he was dispatched to India to serve with the 6th Battalion of the South Wales Borderers.

Lewis' poems about the war and his experiences certainly relay and explore many facets. His poetry is testament to his talents that have him rightly regarded as one of Britain's most promising War Poets albeit on the thinnest of publications.

By 1944 he was a lieutenant in Burma fighting the Japanese. What followed next has been interpreted in several ways. On 5th March 1944 he was found, with a gun shot wound to the head, near the officer's toilets. One account says he had been washing and shaving and then, it seems, tripped and accidentally shot himself. Indeed, that was the official version written up by the army. Another, and perhaps more plausible account classes it as a suicide, the gun was still in his hand. Fatally wounded he survived for another 6 hours.

Whatever the truth as to how or why Alun Lewis died on March 5th, 1944. He was 28.

Index of Contents

The common people do not understand poetry, are shy of poetry, and though they have been taught to admire the true poets of the past are loath to admit that the race is not yet extinct. This is why very little work by living poets has a wide circulation except what is comfortably third-hand and third-rate. The people are not to be blamed: their difficulty is that despite all the charlatans, racketeers and incompetents who have disgraced the poetic profession, an aroma of holiness still clings to the title 'poet', as it does to the titles 'saint' and 'hero', both of which are properly reserved for the dead. It is only when death releases the true poet from the embarrassing condition of being at once immortal and alive in the flesh that the people are prepared to honour him; and his spirit as it passes is saluted by a spontaneous display of public emotion. This explains the heavy black headlines in the Press of March 1944: ALUN LEWIS THE POET IS DEAD. Search the back-files and you will find no preparatory announcement: ALUN LEWIS WRITES GREAT POETRY.
An ancient Triad runs:

Three sacred things:
Poets, groves, kings.

—for an ancient Wales or Ireland a poet was not merely a professional verse-writer: he was acknowledged to exercise extraordinary spiritual power. His person was sacrosanct, like that of the king with whose well-being and well-doing the prosperity of the kingdom was magically bound up, or like the seven prime trees of the sacred grove. When he died the people felt a sudden loss of power and a sorrow stole over them all, even over those who were incapable of understanding the meaning of his simplest poems.

So again now. For Alun Lewis's presence conveyed this same sense of power, which he seemed to have inherited from the commanding poets of his own country. Llywatch Hen, Taliesin, Davydd ap Gwillym and the rest. His friends have described it as both illuminating and healing. I was his friend only by correspondence, but from the start became aware of the power and knew that it lay in his poetic integrity. In 1941 while he was still stationed in England he wrote to me of the difficulty of reconciling his life as a poet with his life as a soldier, and on the difficulty too of knowing where he stood critically and philosophically in a world that was changing its coat so fast. However, he summed up: 'But at any rate I know where I stand in love'-and love is the orientation of every true poet.

In 1942 he was sent to India, a country which at the best of times tries love almost beyond endurance. He found it visited by war, famine and political distress. Though he preserved his integrity he felt tortured: he wrote to a friend 'My insides are haggard'. And when he came to make a collection of his new poems—the ones in this book—he was undecided whether they came up to the standard of accomplishment he had set for them.

I was living safely in England, and my soldiering had finished twenty-five years previously; so he asked me to read the manuscript and decide for him how much should be included and whether any re-writing was needed. In doubtful cases his wife Gweno was to have the casting vote.

It was an embarrassing charge, but guessing how he felt I accepted it. Since this was to be a second book-Raiders' Dawn was the first—it should include, I considered, only his maturest work.
His answer to the suggestion I sent him makes a natural foreword to the book. He wrote it when on the point of going to Burma and it reached me a day or two before his death in Arakan, close to where my eldest son had been killed. Alun was twenty eight years old.

214565 Lieut. A. Lewis,
6th Bn. South Wales Borderers,
India command.

23rd January 1944

Dear Robert,
I've just sent off the bundle of fifty poems in typescript to England by sea mail, and I'm mentally sitting back and contemplating the bony carcase of the demolished fowl. To steady myself I've got your long list of comments and criticism and this is in the nature of an apology for one thing and another.

I was a bit bothered lest the poems and your notes arrived too late for me to do the necessary revising: but I've just managed it in the nick. For both your purgative criticism and your general fiat I am more grateful than I can say.

I won't know your real opinion of my work until you've seen the book as I sent it off. It's substantially as you advised, but I've added some new poems also. The main decision your remarks compelled me to make was over the two very personal love-poems-'Love Letter' and 'Letter from the Cape'. I couldn't decide myself-they are too much flesh of my flesh for me to pretend to assess them: and I've left it to Gweno to exclude them if she chooses. I myself feel that they are necessary to the book: they establish certain things about myself which belong organically to the poems as a whole. In these days of clinical criticism I feel it's as well to tell the world I'm not suffering from a castration or an Œdipus complex and that I'm not writing my head off about thwarted sex-urges. The degree to which a volume of poems should be autobiographical is always different for different people. For myself I can't claim as much hold on the universal as some poets and consider my poems as expressions of personal experience.

[Gweno Lewis decided to exclude the poems, but only when his first resolute attitude about them weakened.]

The shorter poems I've dealt with mainly as you suggested. I've cut the 'moral' endings out and the punk poems like The Reply which you spotted at once. Jason and Medea I've cut in half and to the last verse I've simply added:

And in a nest of snakes he courted her.

I live a certain rhythm which I'm becoming able to recognize. Periods of spiritual death, periods of neutrality, periods of a sickening normality and insane indifference to the real implications of the present, and then for a brief wonderful space, maybe every six weeks, a nervous and powerful ability moves upward in me. India and the army both tend to fortify and protract the negative and passive phase, and if I am suddenly excited and moved by something I have seen or felt, the excitement merely bounces on the hard unchanging surface like a rubber ball on asphalt. I think I'm most completely normal when I'm roaring across the country on a motor-bike, aware of the flow and the tradition of peasant life, passing gay funerals with beautifully attired corpses propped up on canopied platforms, or when I'm peeping at Victorian-Gothic princely palaces in corrupt Native State towns, or eating a coconut in a jungle village in communion with the dancing and chanting you the before the pot-bellied elephant-god of luck.

I've felt a number of things deeply out here; perhaps the jungle has moved me more deeply than anything else, the green wilderness where one has nothing but one's sense of direction and there. is no alarm because there is the Sun and there is one's shadow and there is time-but when I wrote a poem about the jungle I found it had become a criticism of the Western world which in a measure I understand, but of the jungle I had said nothing. That happens nowadays with most of me. And I will have to abandon the vast for the particular, the infinite for the finite, the heart for the eye. A few months ago I refused promotion to a Staff Intelligence job because I wanted something more: I wanted to fuse finite and infinite, in action. I want to go East and East and East, faire le tour; there is a consummation somewhere. After it is over, then I can be particular and exact; meanwhile I learn to fire a revolver with either hand and try to suppress the natural apprehensions of the flesh as a thing so long delayed and postponed and promised and threatened.

'I've taken a sardonic title for the poems from Job 39. 'Ha! Ha! Among the Trumpets'. You know the beautiful chapter. The liberty of the wild ass, the loveliness of the ostrich, the intrepidity of the horse. 'These are the particulars. The Infinite, of which I can never be sure, is God the Maker. I prefer the Ostrich's eggs warming in the sun. I avoid speculations and haven't been touched by intuitions. No attempt has been made to convince me—neither by man nor God. And I'm as restless and fidgety as a man on a deserted platform.

. . . England is 'easy' compared with India—easier to corrupt and easier to improve. There are few deterrents at home: the inclination isn't continually oppressed by the cosmic disinclination, the individual isn't so ruthlessly and permanently subject to the laissez faire of the sun and the sterility. India! What a test of a man!

I hope, when this reaches you, that I'll be about it and about . . . .
So long!
ALUN.

The letter ends with a perfect example of poetic wit: the ingenious smuggling of a concealed meaning into an innocently casual statement. The manifest meaning is: 'I shall soon be about the real business of war. We have had our marching orders. Good-bye until I next write'. The concealed meaning rests on the Fitzgerald quotation read in the light of what he has just written about his religious uncertainty:

Myself when young did eagerly frequent
Doctor and saint and heard great argument
About it and about; but evermore
Came back by the same door as in I went.

He is saying: 'In Burma the problem of the nature of life and death will become still more pressing'. The 'So long' is deceptive too. He had written to his wife about a poem which did not satisfy him:

'I can't reach it—do you see how a poem is made or fails? By perpetual trying, by closer pointing, by seeking and not finding and still seeking, by a robustness in the core of sadness.'

The 'So long' is the robustness in the core of sadness. The manifest meaning is a robustly casual good-bye; the concealed meaning is a sad comment on the years that he has spent in seeking and not finding, and still seeking.

This is how he was writing to his wife about his work in general:

' ... I feel the restlessness and the scattered gift in me and the capacity to suffer and to endure and to persist in the effort to make a unity of all that has been given to me and all that the world casts down upon me.

' ... My longing is more and more for one thing only, integrity, and I discount the other qualities in people ruthlessly if they lack that fundamental sincerity and wholeness.

'. . . I've put a huge burden on you always through my poems which have spoken more openly of the danger and jeopardies than either of us could and would with the living voice. I don't want them to mean foreboding to you or to me. They're universal statements if they're anything. They feel the world and they mean all that is involved in what is happening'.

But then in the consciousness of failure which is the proof of the true poet:

'. . . And although I'm more engrossed with the single poetic theme of Life and Death, for there doesn't seem to be any 'question more directly relevant than this one, of what survives of all the beloved, I find myself quite unable to express at once the passion of Love, the coldness of Death (Death is cold), and the fire that beats against resignation, "acceptance". Acceptance seems so spiritless, protest so vain. In between the two I live'.

GALMPTON, BRIXHAM

1944

ROBERT GRAVES

PART ONE: ENGLAND

I

DAWN ON THE EAST COAST

From Orford Ness to Shingle Street
The grey disturbance spreads
Washing the icy seas on Deben Head,

Cock pheasants scratch the frozen fields,
Gulls lift thin horny legs and step
Fastidiously among the rusted mines.

The soldier leaning on the sandbagged wall
Hears in the combers' curling rush and crash
His single self-centred monotonous wish;

And time is a froth of such transparency
His drowning eyes see what they wish to see;
A girl laying his table with a white cloth.

The light assails him from a flank,

Two carbons touching in his brain
Crumple the cellophane lanterns of his dream

And then the day, grown femimine and kind,
Stoops with the gulfing motion of the tide
And pours his ashes in a tiny urn.

From Orford Ness to Shingle Street
The grey disturbance lifts its head
And one by one, reluctantly,
The living come back slowly from the dead.

II

CORPE CASTLE

Framed in a jagged window of grey stones
These wooded pastures have a dream-like air.
You thrill with disbelief
To see the cattle move in a green field.

Grey Purbeck houses by the sun deceived
Sleep with the easy conscience of the old;
The swathes are sweet on slopes new harvested;
Householders prune their gardens, count the slugs;
The beanrows flicker flowers red as flames.

Those to whom life is a picture card
Get their cheap thrill where here the centuries stand
A thrusting mass transfigured by the sun
Reeling above the streets and crowing farms.
The rooks and skylarks are okay for sound,
The toppling bastions innocent with stock.

Love grows impulsive here: the best forget;
The failures of the earth will try again.
She would go back to him if he but asked.

The tawny thrush is silent: when he sings
His silence is fulfilled. Who wants to talk
As trippers do? Yet, love,
Before we go be simple as this grass.
Lie rustling for this last time in my arms.
Quicken the dying island with your breath.

III

COMPASSION

She in the hurling night
With lucid simple hands
Stroked away his fright
Loosed his bloodsoaked bands

And seriously aware
Of the terror she caressed
Drew his matted hair
Gladly to her breast.

And he who babbled Death
Shivered and grew still
In the meadows of her breath
Restoring his dark will.

Nor did she ever stir
In the storm's calm centre
To feel the tail, hooves, fur
Of the god-faced Centaur.

IV

A WELSH NIGHT

Fine flame of silver birches flickers
Along the coal-tipped misty slopes
Of old Garth mountain who tonight
Lies grey as a sermon of patience
For the threadbare congregations of the anxious.
Huddled in black-out rows the streets
Hoard the hand-pressed human warmth
Of families round a soap-scrubbed table;
Munition girls with yellow hands
Clicking bone needles over khaki scarves,
Schoolboys' painful numerals in a book,
A mother's chilblained fingers soft
Upon the bald head of a suckling child,
But no man in the house to clean the grate
Or bolt the outside door or share the night.
Yet everywhere through cracks of light
Faint strokes of thoughtfulness feel out
Into the throbbing night's malevolence,
And turn its hurt to gentler ways.

Hearing the clock strike midnight by the river
This village buried deeper than the corn
Bows its blind head beneath the angelic planes,

And cherishing all known and suffered harm
It wears the darkness like a shroud or shawl.

V

WESTMINSTER ABBEY

Discoloured lights slant from the high rose window
Upon the sightseers and the faithful
And those who shelter from the rain this Sunday.
The clergy in their starched white surplices
Send prayers like pigeons circling overhead
Seeking the ghostly hands that give them bread.

The togaed statesmen on their scribbled plinths
Stand in dull poses, dusty as their fame
Crammed in the chapter of a schoolboy's 'book:
Their eyes have lost their shrewd and fallible look.

Kneeling by Gladstone is a girl who sobs.
Something profounder than the litany
Moves in the dark beneath the restless steps
Of this pale swirl of human flux.
Soft fingers touch the worn marmoreal stone.
The pale girl reaches out for what has gone.

The thin responsions falter in the air.
Only the restless footsteps hurry on,
Escaping that which was in the beginning,
Is now, and ever shall be.

                              —See, the girl
Adjusts her fashionable veil.
The vergers clack their keys; the soldiers go,
The white procession shuffles out of sight.

The incubus is shifted to the stars,
The flux is spun and drifted through the night,
And no one stays within that holy shell
To know if that which IS be good or ill.

VI

JASON AND MEDEA

The night appeared to authorise it.
The snakes were curling in her tallow hair,

And he stood in the weak and fascinating
Parlour of singing sexes, debonair,
Knowing her hungry glance, her. cool attraction,
The cheap and placid aroma of her smile.
Tomorrow was a carton of abstraction,
A little debt he always could defer.
And in a nest of snakes he courted her.

INFANTRY

By day these men ask nothing, and obey;
They eat their bread behind a heap of stones;
Hardship and violence grow an easy way;
Winter is like a girl within their bones.

They learn the gambits of the soul,
Think lightly of the themes of life and death,
All mortal anguish shrunk into an ache
Too nagging to be worth the catch of breath.

Sharing Life's iron rations, marching light,
Enduring to the end the early cold,
The emptiness of noon, the void of night
In whose black market they are bought and sold;
They take their silent stations for the fight.
Rum's holy unction makes the dubious bold,

SONG

I lay in sheets of softest linen
Sleepless and my lover spoke
The word of Death within her sleep
And snuggled closer and awoke
And wrapped me in her snow-white cloak,

And clasped me in exhausted arms
And swore I should not go again.
Her lips were writhing like a moth
Burnt in the steady lamp of pain.

I heard the daylight wind its horn,
I saw the cloudy horsemen ride.
But my beloved lacked the strength

To keep me by her side
And I went forth in pride

I clasped the burning sun all day,
The cold moon bled me white;
Then all things ended suddenly.
I saw the world take flight
And glitter in the starry night.

IX

ENCIRCLEMENT

Wrapped in the night's diseases,
Haunted by streetwalking fancies
Of Coty and hunchbacks and sequins,
In the nameless dugouts and basements
Of Everyman's darkness,
I seek in the distant footfalls
The elusive answer of love,
Till deeper than any appearance
Or any one man's failure,
The shrivelled roots touch water.

And on this abandoned frontier
Where many visions falter
And youth and health are taken
Without complaint or reason,
I strive with the heart's blind strength
 To reach the mild and patient place
Where the lamplit room awaits a stranger
And suffering has sanctified your face.

X

SONG

Oh journeyman, Oh journeyman,
Before this endless belt began
Its cruel revolutions, you and she
Naked in Eden shook the apple tree.

Oh soldier lad, Oh soldier lad,
Before the soul of things turned bad,
She offered you so modestly
A shining apple from the tree.

Oh lonely wife, Oh lonely wife,
Before your lover left this life
He took you in his gentle arms.
How trivial then were Life's alarms.

And though Death taps down every street
Familiar as the postman 'on his beat,
Remember this, Remember this
That Life has trembled in a kiss
From Genesis to Genesis,

And what's transfigured will live on
Long after Death has come and gone

II

THE CRUCIFIXION

From the first he would not avoid it.
He knew they would stone and defile him, and looked to it calmly,
Riding to meet it serenely across the palm leaves,
Processions in the East being near to bloodshed,
Foreseeing a time when the body and all its injunctions
And life and people and all their persistent demands
Would desist, and they'd leave a policeman
Outside his door or his tomb to keep all in order
While he lay in supremest consummate passion
Passively passionate, suffering suffering only.

And this surrender of self to a greater statement
Has been desired by many more humble than he.
But when it came, was it other than he had imagined?
Breaking his Self up, convulsing his Father in pain?
His will prevented by every throbbing stigma,
The pangs that puffed and strained his stomach wall,
The utter weariness that bowed his head,
Taught him perhaps that more hung on the presence
Of all the natural preoccupations,
Duties, emotions, daily obligations
Affections and responses than he'd guessed.
They'd grown a burden to him, but as a mother
 Is burdened by her child's head when her breasts
Are thin and milkless; he knew this awful hanging
Obscene with urine, sagging on a limb,
Was not the end of life, and improved nothing.

SACCO WRITES TO HIS SON

I did not want to die. I wanted you,
You and your sister Inez and your mother.
Reject this death, my Dante, seek out Life,
Yet not the death-in-life that most men live.
My body aches ... I think I hear you weep.
You must not weep. . . . Tears are a waste of strength.
Seven years your mother wept, not as your mother,
But as my wife; So make her more your mother.
Take her the ways I know she can escape
From the poor soulness that so wearies her.
Take her into the country every Sunday,
Ask her the name of such and such a plant,
Gather a basket each of herbs and flowers,
Ask her to find the robin where he nests,
She will be happy then. Tears do no damage
That spring from gladness, though they scald the throat.
Go patiently about it. Not too much
Just yet, Dante, good boy. You'll know.

And for yourself, remember in the play
Of happiness you must not act alone.
Husband yourself, but never stale your mind
With prudence or with doubting. I could wish
You saw my body slipping from the chair
Tomorrow. You'd remember that, my son,
And would not weigh the cost of our struggle
Against the product as a poor wife does.
But I'll not break your sleep with such a nightmare.
You looked so happy when you lay asleep. . .

But I have neither strength nor room for all
These thoughts. One single thought's enough
To fill immensity. I drop my pen . . .

I hope this letter finds you in good health,
My son, my comrade. Will you give my love
To Inez and your mother and my friends.
Bartolo also sends his greetings to you.
I would have written better and more simple
Except my head spins like a dancing top
And my hand trembles . . . I am Oh, so weak . . .

XIII

GOODBYE

So we must say Goodbye, my darling,
And go, as lovers go, for ever;
Tonight remains, to pack and fix on labels
And make an end of lying down together.

I put a final shilling in the gas,
And watch you slip your dress below your knees
And lie so still I hear your rustling comb
Modulate the autumn in the trees.

And all the countless things I shall remember
Lay mummy-cloths of silence round my head;
I fill the carafe with a drink of water;
You say "We paid a guinea for this bed,"

And then, "We'll leave some gas, a little warmth
For the next resident, and these dry flowers,"
And turn your face away, afraid to speak
The big word, that Eternity is ours.

Your kisses close my eyes and yet you stare
As though God struck a child with nameless fears;
Perhaps the water glitters and discloses
Time's chalice and its limpid useless tears.

Everything we renounce except our selves;
Selfishness is the last of all to go;
Our sighs are exhalations of the earth,
Our footprints leave 'a track across the snow.

We made the universe to be our home,
Our nostrils took the wind to be our breath,
Our hearts are massive towers of delight,
We stride across the seven seas of death.

Yet when all's done you'll keep the emerald
I placed upon your finger in the street;
And I will keep the patches that you sewed
On my old battledress tonight, my sweet.

PART TWO: THE VOYAGE

THE DEPARTURE

Eyes closed, half waking, that first morning
He felt the curved grey bows enclose him,
The voyage beginning, the oceans giving way
To the thrust of steel, the pulse and beat
Of the engines that even now were revolving,

Revolving, rotating, throbbing along his brain
Rattling the hurried carpentry of his bunk,
Setting an unknown bearing into space.

He never thought that he might doubt or fear
Or lose himself or kill an honest man
Or die in some street outrage. Always there
Beneath the exertion and the novelty
Would be the deep sad rhythm of the process
Of the created thing awaking to the sound of the engine.

And he remembered all that was prevented,
How she came with him to the barrier
And knowing she could come no further
Turned back on the edge of his sleep,
Vexed, fumbling in her handbag,
Giving the world a dab of rouge and powder,
A toss of head, a passing hatred,
Going in all these trivial things, yet proudly;

Knowing more deeply than he the threat of his voyage,
With all a living woman's fear of death.

He heard the seagulls crying round the porthole
And in his sleepy trouble he knew the chafing
Of nettles her hands would be weaving into a garment
To turn her white-winged lover back to man,
A man released from the weary fluctuations
Of time and distance, forgetfulness and dying.

And then he woke unrested from his longing,
And locked himself and hurried to offload
Boxes of ammunition from the wagons
And send them swaying from the groaning derricks
Deep into the unrefusing ship.

XV

ON EMBARKATION

Consider this silent disciplined assembly
Close squadded in the dockyard's hooded lamps,
Each blur a man with some obscure trouble
Or hard regret as bulky as the cargo
The cranking derricks drop into the hold.
Think of them, as the derrick sways and poises
Vacantly as their minds do at this passage,
Good-natured agents of a groping purpose
That sends them now to strange precipitous places

Where all are human and Oh easily hurt
And—the temptation being to forget
Such villages as linger in the mind,

Lidice on the road from. Bethlehem—
Ask whether kindness will persist in hearts
Plagued by the snags and rapids of a curse,
And whether the fortunate few will still attain
The sudden flexible grasp of a dangerous problem
And feel their failures broaden into manhood,
Or take the Bren's straightforward road
And grow voluptuous at the sight of blood?
Each of us is invisible to himself,
Our eyes grow neutral in the long Unseen,
We take or do not take a hand of cards,
We shake down nightly in the strange Unknown.
yet each one has a hankering in the blood,
A dark relation that disturbs his joke
And will not be abandoned with a shrug:
Each has a shrunken inkling of the Good.
And one man, wrapped in blankets, solemnly
Remembers as he bites his trembling nails
The white delightful limbs, the nest of peace.
And one who misses what it's all about,
Sick with injections, sees the 'tween-decks turn
To fields of home, each tree with its rustling shadow
Slipped like a young girl's dress down to its ankles;
Where lovers lay in chestnut shadows,
And horses came there from the burning meadows.
And these things stay, in seasonal rotation
Within the cycles of our false intention.

But others, lacking the power of reflection,
Broke ship, impelled by different emotions.
The police are seeking men of their description
As sedulously as their own promotion.

II

Before he sails a man may go on leave
To any place he likes, where he's unknown
Or where he's mentioned with a warm inflection
And hands are shaken up and down the street.
Some men avoid this act of recognition
And make the world a dartboard for their fling;
Oblivion is the colour of brown ale;
Peace is the backseat in the cinema.
But most men seek the place where they were born.

For me it was a long slow day by train.

Just here you leave this Cardiganshire lane,
Here by these milk churns and this telegraph pole;
Latch up the gate and cut across the fields.
Some things you see in detail, those you need;
The raindrops spurting from the trodden stubble
Squirting your face across the reaping meadow,
The strange machine-shaped scarab beetle
His scalloped legs clung bandy to a stalk,
The Jew's-harp bee with saddlebags of gold,
The wheat as thin as hair on flinty slopes,
The harsh hewn faces of the farming folks,
Opinion humming like a nest of wasps,
The dark-clothed brethren at the chapel gates;
And farther on the mortgaged crumbling farm
Where Shonni Rhys, that rough backsliding man
Has found the sheep again within the corn
And fills the evening with his sour oaths;
The curse of failure's in his shambling gait.

At last the long wet sands, the shelving beach,
The green Atlantic, far as eye can reach.
And what is here but what was always here
These twenty years, elusive as a dream
Flowing between the grinding-stones of fact—
A girl's affections or. a new job lost,
A lie that burns the soft stuff in the brain,
Lust unconfessed, a scholarship let go
Or gained too easily, without much point—
Each hurt a search for those old country gods
A man takes with him in his native tongue
Finding a friendly word for all things strange,
The firm authentic truth of roof and rain.
And on the cliff's green brink where nothing stirs,
Unless the wind should stir it, I perceive
A child grow shapely in the loins I love.

III

In all the ways of going who can tell
The real from the unjustified farewell?
Women have sobbed when children left for school
Or husbands took the boat train to pursue
Contracts more tenuous than the marriage vow.
But now each railway station makes and breaks
The certain hold and drifts us all apart,
Some women know exactly what's implied.
Ten Years, they say · behind their smiling eyes,
Thinking of children, pensions, looks that fade,
The slow forgetfulness that strips the mind

Of its apparel and wears down the thread;
Or maybe when he laughs and bends to make

Her laugh with him she sees that he must die
Because his eyes declare it plain as day.
And it is here, if anywhere, that words
-Debased like money by the same diseases—
Cast off the habitual cliches of fatigue
-The women hoping it will soon blow over,
The fat men saying it depends on Russia—
And all are poets when they say Goodbye
And what they say will live and fructify.

IV

And so we wait the tide, and when the dark
Laps round the swelling entrance to the sea
The grey evasive ship slips into line.
The bell clangs in the engine room, the night
Shrouds the cold faces watching at the rail.
Till suddenly from headland and from wharves
The searchlights throw their lambent bluish cloaks
Clothing the fairway in a sheen of silk.
The steel bows break, the churning screw burns white.
Each pallid face wears an unconscious smile.
And I-I pray my unborn tiny child
Has five good senses and an earth as kind
As the sweet breast of her who gives him milk
And waves me down this first clandestine mile.

XVI

A TROOPSHIP IN THE TROPICS

Five thousand souls are here and all are bounded
Too easily perhaps by the ostensible purpose,
Steady as the ploughshare cleaving England,
Of this great ship, obedient to its compass.

The sundeck for the children and the officers
Under the awning, watching the mid-sea blue
Until the nurses pass with a soft excitement
Rustling the talk of passengers and crew.

Deep in the foetid holds the tiered bunks
Hold restless men who sweat and toss and sob;
The gamblers on the hatches, in the corner
The accordionist and barber do their job.

The smell of oranges and excrement
Moves among those who write uneasy letters
Or slouch about and curse the stray dejection
That chafes them with its hard nostalgic fetters.

But everywhere in this sweltering Utopia,
In the bareheaded crowd's two minutes' silence,
In corners where the shadows lie like water,
Are tranquil pools of crystal-clear reflexion.

Time is no mystery now; this torrid blueness
Blazed in a fortnight from the English winter.
Distance is subject to our moods and wishes.
Only the void of feeling must be filled

And as the ship makes peace within herself
The simple donors of goodness with rugged features
Move in the crowd and share their crusts of wisdom;
Life does not name her rough undoctored teachers.

Welsh songs surge softly in the circling darkness;
Thoughts sail back like swans to the English winter;
Strange desires drift into the mind;
Time hardens. But the ruthless Now grows kind.

XVII

CHANSON TRISTE

By day the sun ranted
Strode to his zenith'
Stared imperturbably
Pitiless conqueror.

And the moon in her gentleness
Softly companions us
Leading us, wayfarers,
Through her white acres.

But how can we sleep
Though the hour is late,
Who lost man's fine mastery
Over his fate?

With all that is human
The tall stars decline.
Bitterest agony
Bleeds the divine.

And huge as the shadows
My longing runs wild
Oh world! Oh wanton!
For my woman, my child.

SONG

(On seeing dead bodies floating off the Cape)

The first month of his absence
I was numb and sick
And where he'd left his promise
Life did not turn or kick.
The seed, the seed of love was sick.

The second month my eyes were sunk
In the darkness of despair,
And my bed was like a grave
And his ghost was lying there.
And my heart was sick with care.

The third month of his going
I thought I heard him say
"Our course deflected slightly
On the thirty-second day—"
The tempest blew his words away.

And he was lost among the waves,
His ship rolled helpless in the sea,
The fourth month of his voyage
He shouted grievously
"Beloved, do not think of me."

The flying fish like kingfishers
Skim the sea's bewildered crests,
The whales blow steaming fountains,
The seagulls have no nests
Where my lover sways and rests.

We never thought to buy and sell
This life that blooms or, withers in the leaf,
And I'll not stir, so he sleeps well,
Though cell by cell the coral reef
Builds an eternity of grief.

But oh! the drag and dullness of my Self;

The turning seasons wither in my head;
All this slowness, all this hardness,
The nearness that is waiting in my bed,
The gradual self-effacement of the dead.

PORT OF CALL: BRAZIL

We watch the heavy-odoured beast
Of darkness crouch along the water-front
Under the town exorcised by the priest.
The lights entice the paramours to hunt.

Tropical thunder creams the glassy bay,
White sails on bamboo masts disturb the night,
The troopship turns and drags upon her stay,
The portholes cast a soft, subjective light.

And we who crowd in hundreds to the side
Feel the lights prick us with a grey distaste
As though we had some guilty thing to hide
We, who thought the negroes were debased

This morning when they scrambled on the quay
For what we threw, and from their dugout boats
Haggled cigars and melons raucously
Lifting their bleating faces like old goats.

But now the white-faced tourist must translate
His old unsated longing to adventure
Beyond the European's measured hate.
Into the dangerous oceans of past and future

Where trembling intimations will reveal
The illusion of this blue mulatto sleep
And in that chaos like a migrant eel
Will breed a new direction through the deep.

PART THREE: INDIA

TO RILKE

Rilke, if you had known that I was trying

To speak to you perhaps you would have said
"Humanity has her darlings to whom she's entrusted
A farthing maybe, or a jewel, at least a perception
Of what can develop and what must be always endured
And what the live may answer to the dead.
Such ones are known by their faces,
At least their absence is noted;
And they never lack an occasion,
They, the devoted."

But I have to seek the occasion.
Labour, fatigue supervene;
The glitter of sea and land, the self-assertion
These fierce competing times insist upon.

Yet sometimes, seeking, hours glided inwards,
Laying their soft antennae on my heart,
And I forgot the thousand leagues I'd journeyed
As if Creation were about to start.

I watched the pure horizon for the earth
To rise in grey bare peaks that might enfold
The empty crumbling soil between the hands

Or coloured things a child's small fist might hold
Delightedly; I knew that unknown lands
Were near and real, like an act of birth.

Then I fell ill and restless.
Sweating and febrile all one burning week,
I hungered for the silence you acquired
And envied you, as though it were a gift
Presented on a birthday to the lucky.
For that which IS I thought you need not seek.

The sea. is gone now and the crowded tramp
Sails other seas with other passengers.
I sit within the tent, within the darkness
Of India, and the wind disturbs my lamp.

The jackals howl and whimper in the nullah,
The goatherd sleeps upon a straw-piled bed,
And I know that in this it does not matter
Where one may be or what fate lies ahead.

And Vishnu, carved by some rude pious hand,
Lies by a heap of stones, demanding nothing
But the simplicity that she and I
Discovered in a way you'd understand
Once and for ever, Rilke, but in Oh a distant land.

BY THE GATEWAY OF INDIA, BOMBAY

The storm's cold javelins constrain
The swirling roads, the anchored fleet
Curled in Elephanta's lee
Where pilgrims walked on naked feet:
—And in the darkness did they see
The darker terrors of the brain?
And did the hollow oracle resound
In caves of unexpected pain?
And were they drenched· as we who loiter
Beneath the Imperial Gate
By the biting arrows of the rain?
And did they also hate?

We who let the evening come
Have our peculiar pride, never to flinch;
Our dignity has schooled us to submit:
Life has withdrawn its word, the day has gone,
But we contest the darkness inch by inch.
And though the starving outcasts tell
The imminent peril of the state
We are incredulous of fate.

A red-winged gull beats down the bay,
Finds the mole, the square of green,
And shakes the tempest off its breast.
But we who with the beggars lean
Against the indifferent arch of kings
Infected with the crowd's unrest
And remembering younger springs,
Tie the aching knots of lust
In the harlot's clinging breath,
Knowing life and knowing death.

THE WAY BACK

Six days and two thousand miles
I have watched the shafted rain
Feminise the burning land,
Cloaking with a green distress
The cerulean and the ochre
Of the season's 'ruthlessness.

Six days and two thousand miles
I have gone alone
With a green mind and you
Burning in the stubborn bone.

Soldiers quickened by your breath
Feel the sudden spur and rush
Of the life they put away
Lest the war should break and crush
Beauties more profound than death.

I swam within your naked lake
And breasted with exquisite ease
The foaming arabesques of joy
And in the sarabande of trees
Of guava and papaya
And crimson blown poinsettia,
The millrace of my blood
Beat against my smile,
And were you answering my smile
Or the millrace of my blood?

But now the iron beasts deploy
And all my effort is my fate
With gladiators and levies
All laconic disciplined men
I pass beyond your golden gate.

And in the hardness of this world
And in the brilliance of this pain
I exult with such a passion
To be squandered, to be hurled,
To be joined to you again.

XXIII

KARANJE VILLAGE

The sweeper said Karanje had a temple
A roof of gold in the gaon:
But I saw only the long-nosed swine and the vultures
Groping the refuse for carrion,

And the burial cairns on the hill with its spout of dust
Where the mules stamp and graze,
The naked children begging, the elders in poverty,
The sun's dry beat and glaze,

The crumbling hovels like a discredited fortress,
The old hags mumbling by the well,
The young girls in purple always avoiding us,
The monkeys loping obscenely round our smell—

—The trees were obscene with the monkeys' grey down-hanging
Their long slow leaping and stare,
The girl in a red sari despairingly swinging her rattle,
The sacred monkeys mocking all her care.

And alone by a heap of stones in the lonely salt plain
A little Vishnu of stone,
Silently and eternally simply Being,
Bidding me come alone,

And never entirely turning me away,
But warning me still of the flesh,
That catches and limes the singing birds of the soul
And holds their wings in mesh.

But the people are hard and hungry and have no love
Diverse and alien, uncertain in their hate,
Hard stones flung out of Creation's silent matrix,
And the Gods must wait.

And Love must wait, as the unknown yellow poppy
Whose lovely fragile petals are unfurled
Among the lizards in this wasted land.
And when my sweetheart calls me shall I tell her
That I am seeking less and less of world?
And will she understand?

XXIV

THE MAHRATTA GHATS

The valleys crack and burn, the exhausted plains
Sink their black teeth into the horny veins
Straggling the hills' red thighs, the bleating goats
—Dry bents and bitter thistles in their throats—
Thread the loose rocks by immemorial tracks.
Dark peasants drag the sun upon their backs.

High on the ghat the new turned soil is red,
The sun has ground it to the finest red,
It lies like gold within each horny hand.
Siva has spilt his seed upon this land.

Will she who burns and withers on the plain

Leave, ere too late, her scraggy herds of pain,
The cow-dung fire and the trembling beasts,
The little wicked gods, the grinning priests,
And climb, before a thousand years have fled,
High as the eagle to her mountain bed
Whose soil is fine as flour and blood-red?

But no! She cannot move. Each arid patch
Owns the lean folk who plough and scythe and thatch
Its grudging yield and scratch its stubborn stones.
The small gods suck the marrow from their bones.

Who is it climbs the summit of the road?
Only the beggar bumming his dark load.
Who was it cried to see the falling star?
Only the landless soldier lost in war.

And did a thousand years go by in vain?
And does another thousand start again?

"HOLI"

(The Hindu festival of Spring)

The village is · growing fertile,
The bankrupt peasant feels the wheat
Spring green within his stony loins,
All night the sweating drumsticks beat.

The girls with priestly faces
Stir in the circle of flame.
Red ochre melts on their foreheads,
Their eyes are dark with shame.

The drum beats a crescendo,
The young men are fain,
The moon is swollen in the forest
The young girls twitch with pain.

Blood drips from the drumskins,
The youths and girls obey
The wild God's uttermost intent,
And sob, and turn away,

And turn to the Indian forest
And there they are as one-
One with the dust and darkness

When the God's last will is done.

THE JOURNEY

We were the fore-runners of an army,
Going among strangers without sadness,
Danger being as natural as strangeness.

We had no other urge but to compel
Tomorrow in the image of today,
Which was· motion and mileage and tinkering.
When cylinders mis-fired and the gasket leaked.
Distance exhausted us each night;
I curled up in the darkness like a dog
And being a romantic stubbed my eyes
Upon the wheeling spokeshave of the stars.

Daylight had girls tawny as gazelles,
Beating their saris clean in pools and singing.
When we stopped they covered up their breasts;
Sometimes their gestures followed us for miles.

Then caravanserais of gipsies
With donkeys grey as mice and mincing camels
Laden with new-born lambs and trinkets,
Tentage and utensils and wicker baskets,
Following the ancient routes of the vast migrations
When history was the flight of a million birds
And poverty had splendid divagations.

Sometimes there were rivers that refused us,
Sweeping away the rafts, the oxen;
Some brown spates we breasted.
The jungle let us through with compass and machets.
And there were men like fauns, with drenched eyes,
Avoiding us, bearing arrows.

There was also the memory of Death
And the recurrent irritation of our selves.
But the wind so wound its ways about us,
Beyond this living and this loving,
This calculation and provision, this fearing,
That neither of us heard the quiet voice calling us,
Remorse like rain softening and rotting the ground,
We felt no sorrow in the singing bird,
Forgot the sadness we had left behind.
For how could we guess, oh Life, oh suffering and patient Life,

With distance spun for ever in the mind,
We among the camels, the donkeys and the waterfalls,
How could we ever guess,
Not knowing how you pined?

WAYS

I

It had been easier, not loving.

I knew I had grown harder than the trees
In which I held you all the afternoon,
The tall blue slender saplings leaning
Each on each, their strength outgrowing.
And suddenly we two were swaying
Each upon the other leaning.

It had been easier, not loving.

II

It was much easier, all alone.

The tall slim saplings were exhausted so
With tallness and with slenderness they bowed
At the touch of wind or bird.
And the lightness of your hands
Bowed me also with their guerdon,
Love being gravel in the wound

When the silent lovers know
Swaying in the misty rain
The old oppression of the burden
Growing in them as they go,
Though trees are felled and grow again,
Far and farther each from each.
Longing hardens like a stone.

Lovers go but hardly, all alone.

XXVIII

VILLAGE FUNERAL: MAHARASHTRA

The wasted sleepy corpse
Benignly, unassumingly reposes
Among the flowers flung on him all day.
The cow-dung fire decomposes.

The drum denies identity,
The patient elements ignite,
Life stirs and shifts and gradually breaks
Within the burning night.

This dead man is no more.
Silence fills the throbbing drum,
Dries the sweat on every face,
Mutely bids the· dayspring come.

Nandi, bull of holiness,
Ganpati, elephantine force,
Siva, destroyer and sparer,
Consider this poor corpse.

Not being and then being,
Cow-dung fire, bed of earth,—
How shall the peasant fare between
One birth and another birth?

XXIX

WATER MUSIC

Deep in the heart of the lake
Where the last light is clinging
A strange foreboding voice
Is patiently singing.

Do not fear to venture
Where the last light trembles
Because you were in love.
Love never dissembles.

Fear no more the boast, the bully,
The lies, the vain labour.
Make no show for death
As for a rich neighbour.

What stays of the great religions?
An old priest, an old birth.
What stays of the great battles?
Dust on the earth.

Cold is the lake water
And dark as history.
Hurry not and fear not
This oldest mystery.

This strange voice singing,
This slow deep drag of the lake,
This yearning, yearning, this ending
Of the heart and its ache.

XXX

SHADOWS

The moon turns round the earth
And the earth turns round the sun;
In gold and white infinities
Their timeless task is done.

Under the shadow of the earth
The moon in crescent stays,
Dark as an untended wound
Despite the splendid phrase.

Love reeled in that dark, and beauty
Stained the rocks with fragile flowers.
But love and beauty will survive
These grey malignant hours.

Strangeness does not make me strange.
Of strangers born I know that good
Lay with evil in the hedge.
The rest is in the mood.

He chooses best who does not choose
Time and all its lies;
Who makes the end and the beginning One
Within himself, grows wise.

The cold winds of indifference
Disturb the scarves of night,
As earth and moon go voyaging
Through dark, through light.

XXXI

HOME THOUGHTS FROM ABROAD

As if the ant should fail with desire
And cast her chiffon wings and groan,
The trumpet's warm and selfish lusts
Occlude this breathless Indian night.
The trumpeter stands alone.

Oh West, your blue nostalgic moods
Confuse the troubled continents.
The shaven-headed prisoners moan
And girls with serpents at their breasts
And boys with dead hands on their knees
 Lie stricken in your scattered tents.

And we who feel the darkness twitch
With death among the orange trees
Seek, and not in vain, your hills
Whose bridle paths all end in dark
And find love in the gap of centuries
Although the swart brown heather bears no mark
Of boy and girl and all they planned.

We surely were not hard to please
And yet you cast us out. And in this land
We bear the dark inherited disease
Bred in the itching warmness of your hand.

IN HOSPITAL: POONA (I)

I

Last night I did not fight for sleep
But lay awake from midnight while the world
Turned its slow features to the moving deep
Of darkness, till I knew that you were furled,

Beloved, in the same dark watch as I.
And sixty degrees of longitude beside
Vanished as though a swan in ecstasy
Had spanned the distance from your sleeping side.

And like to swan or moon the whole of Wales
Glided within the parish of my care:
I saw the green tide leap on Cardigan,
Your red yacht riding like a legend there,

And the great mountains, Dafydd and Llewelyn,
Plynlimmon, Cader Idris and Eryri

Threshing the darkness back from head and fin,
And also the small nameless mining valley

Whose slopes are.scratched with streets and sprawling graves
Dark in the lap of firwoods and great boulders
Where you lay waiting, listening to the waves-
My hot hands touched your white despondent shoulders

—And then ten thousand miles by daylight grew
Between us, and I heard the wild claws crake
In India's starving throat; whereat I knew
That Time upon the heart can break
But love survives the venom of the snake.

XXXIII

IN HOSPITAL: POONA (II)

The sun has sucked and beat the encircling hills
Into gaunt skeletons; the sick men watch
Soft' shadows warm those bones of rock,
And the barefooted peasants winding back,
Sad withered loins in hanging dirty folds,
Mute sweepings from the disappointed streets,
Old shrunken tribes the starving dusk enfolds.
The wind sweeps up the rifle range and blows
The Parsis' long white robes, there where they go
Under the wheeling kites, bearing a corpse
To the high tower that the vultures know.

And from the polished ward where men lie ill
Thought rubs clean through the frayed cloth of the will,
Piercing the slow estrangement of disease,
And breaks into a state of blinding light
Where Now is a salt pillar, still and white,
And there are no familiar words or features
Nor blood nor tears no joy nor living creatures,
A void where Pain demands no cheap release
But white and rigid freezes into peace,
And mind lies coiled within green icebound streams
And sheds the stippled scales of ancient dreams.

And by that Arctic silence overawed
The mind crawls wounded from the lidless God,
And breeds again the hope that has no food
But lives amongst the evil and the good,
Biding its time amongst the lives that fail
While darkness crowds its dark piratic sail.
Yet in the garden of the hospital

The moonlight spills and sings in a stone pool,
Allowing those who loiter to recall
That which the whiplash sun drove out of bounds—
The heart's calm voice that stills the baying hounds.

INDIAN DAY

Dawn's cold imperative compels
Bazaars and gutters to disturb
Famine's casual ugly tableaux.
Lazarus is lifted from the kerb.

The supple sweeper girl goes by
Brushing the dung of camels from the street
The daylight's silver bangles
Glitter on her naked feet.

II

Yellow ramtilla stiffens in the noon,
Jackals skulk among the screes,
In skinny fields the oxen shiver,
The gods have prophesied disease.

Hedges of spike and rubber, hedges of cactus,
Lawns of bougainvillia, jasmine, zinnia,
Terraces of privelege and loathing,
The masterly shadows of a nightmare

Harden and grow lengthy in the drought.
The moneyed antipathetic faces
Converse in courts of pride and fountains
With ermined sleek injustices.
Gods and dacoits haunt the mountains

III

The sun the thunder and the hunger grow
Extending stupidly the fields of pain
Ploughing the peasant under with his crop
Denying the great mercy of the rain

Denying what each flowering pear and lime
And every child and each embrace imply—
The love that is imprisoned in each heart

By the famines and fortunes of the century.

IV

Night bibles India in her wilderness
The Frontier Mail screams blazing with such terror
The russet tribesman lays aside his flute
Rigid with Time's hypnotic surging error.

The kindness of the heart lies mute
Caught in the impotence of dreams
Yet all night long the, boulders sing
The timeless songs of mountain streams.

XXXV

THE PEASANTS

The dwarf barefooted, chanting
Behind the oxen by the lake,
Stepping lightly and lazily among the thorn-trees
Dusky and dazed with sunlight, half awake;

The women breaking stones upon the highway,
Walking erect with burdens on their heads,
One body growing in another body,
Creation touching verminous straw beds.

Across scorched hills and trampled crops
The soldiers straggle by.
History staggers in their wake.
The peasants watch them die.

XXXVI

OBSERVATION POST: FORWARD AREA

The thorns are bleached and brittle,
The empty folds decay,
Rooftrees creak in the silence
Of inarticulate dismay.

Drought denudes the planting;
In the dry red heat
Dawn spills its ghostly water,
Black heads on the wheat.

Some evil presence quenches
The vagrant drunken theme
Of the swart and skinny goatherd
And the black goats of his dream.

A darker beast than poverty
Transfixed the crouching peasants there,
And tore the votive tablets down
And filled the children with such fear.

The cow-dung fires guttered out,
The wizened women cried,
The bridegroom lay trembling,
And rigid the bride.

Love could be had for nothing.
And where is love now?
Gone with the shambling oxen,
Gone with the broken plough,
Death lives here now.

XXXVII

BURMA CASUALTY

(To Captain G. T. Morris, Indian Army)

Three endless weeks of sniping all the way,
Lying up when their signals rang too close,
—"Ooeee, Ooee," like owls, the lynx-eyed Jap,—
Sleeplessly watching, knifing, falling back.
And now the Sittang river was there at last
And the shambles of trucks and corpses round the bridge
And the bridge was blown. And he laughed.

And then a cough of bullets, a dusty cough
Filleted all his thigh from knee to groin.
The kick of it sucked his face into the wound.
He crumpled, thinking 'Death'. But no, not yet.
 The femoral artery wasn't touched.
Great velour cloaks of darkness floated up.
But he refused, refused the encircling dark,
A lump of bitter gristle that refused.
The day grew bloodshot as they picked him up.

II

Lying in hospital he often thought
Of that darkness, whence it came
And how it played the enchantress in a grain
Of morphia or a nodding of the head
Late in the night and offered to release
The Beast that breathed with pain and ran with pus
Among the jumping fibres of the flesh.
And then he saw the Padre by his cot
With the Last Unction: and he started up.

III

"Your leg must go. Okay?" the surgeon said
"Take it" he said. "I hate the bloody thing."
Yet he was terrified—not of the knives
Nor loosing that green leg (he'd often wished
He'd had a gun to shoot the damned thing off)
But of the darkness that he knew would come
And bid him enter its deep gates alone.

The nurse would help him and the orderlies.
But did they know? And could a rubber tube.
Suck all that darkness out of lungs and heart?

"Open and close your fist—slowly," the doctor said.
He did so, lying still upon his back.
The whitewashed walls, the windows bright with sky
Gathered a brilliant light above his head.
Here was the light, the promise hard and pure,
His wife's sweet body and her wilful eyes.
Her timeless love stooped down to raise him up.
He felt the white walls part-the needle pricked,
"Ten seconds and you'll fade," the doctor said.
He lay and looked into the snow-white skies
For all ten seconds means at such a time.
Then through the warped interstices of life
The darkness swept like water through a boat
In gouts and waves of softness, claiming him ...

He went alone: knew nothing: and returned
Retching and blind with pain, and yet Alive.

IV

Mending, with books and papers and a fan
Sunlight on parquet floors· and bowls of flame
He heard quite casually that his friends were dead,
His regiment too butchered to reform.
And he lay in the lightness of the ward

Thinking of all the lads the dark enfolds So secretly.

And yet a man may walk
Into and through it, and return alive.
Why had his friends all stayed there, then?
He knew.
The dark is a beautiful singing sexless angel

Her hands so soft you - scarcely feel her touch
Gentle, eternally gentle, round your heart.
She flatters and unsexes every man.

And Life is only a crude, pig-headed churl
Frowsy and starving, daring to suffer alone.

XXXVIII

THE UNKNOWN SOLDIER

Everything has lasted· till today.
He stares upon it like a velvet king.
Velasquez might have made this flaccid mask,
The silence round the languid mouth,
The weak and glassy eyes, the crumpled brow.
All things are out-distanced now.

All days are heaped in wrath upon today.
The senses sleep except one crazy spark
That leaps the lesion slashed between his eyes
And cries-not for a fertile century,
Nor for the secular ransom of the soul—
But for a sip of water from my flask. '
What is the soul to him?
He has outlasted everything.

Joy's deceitful liturgy has ceased.
Tomorrow and tomorrow have no place
Among the seas of rain, the seas of peace
That are the elements of this poor face.

The mean humiliating self no more
Has access to him, nor the friends
Whose sensual persuasions first began
The brittle scattering that this day ends.
On pander, lord and jester slams the door.
And impotent in his kingdom the grey king
No longer clings to that which dies.

He has abandoned everything.

Velasquez, close those doglike dolorous eyes.

PEASANT SONG

The seed is costly
Sow it carefully
I have only this small plough
To turn the mighty earth.

And will you kiss me now
And with mysterious birth
Bless this hut of rod and reed
And I will turn the mighty earth
And you will hold the seed?

And if sun and rain are kind
The young green crops will grow
More abundant than my mind
Swaying where the cattle graze

But if I should go
And you be left behind
Among the tall red ant hills and the maize
Would you hear my plough still singing
And, bearing endless days,
Somehow give praise?

WOOD SONG

The pine trees cast their needles softly
Darling for your gipsy bed
And the tall blue saplings swaying
Whisper more than can be said.

Piteously the world is happening
Beyond this cool stockade of trees
Enduring passions penetrate
These quiet rides with agonies
That love can never consummate.

And we must go because we love
Beyond ourselves, beyond these trees
That sway above your golden head

Till wind and war and sky and dove
Become again the murmur of your breath
And your body the white shew-bread.

THE ISLAND

I watched your houseboat, young patrician,
Cast off the island and attempt the bay,
I knew it was no routine trip to purchase
The island's meat and bread for one more day.

Garlanded, you paid away like rope
The island's mastery, only achieved
The moment you forsook it; I discerned
A woman standing dull as the bereaved.

And now the mainland takes you with its hunger
And as your boat jerks crunching on the shore
Do you step off fastidious as a virgin,
Or with the mute complaisance of a whore?

And were you taught what words are expeditious
What sins are venial, what are held in shame?
And 'have you sipped the blue bouquet of power
And were you humble when they promised fame?

How will you meet the first appraising glances
Of the anonymous strangers in the street?
Do you grow fierce within the toils of pity?
And know the millions you will never meet?

And do you in this piteous human flux
Possess the high imponderable art
To turn us by a hair's-breadth in our trouble
To greater agony or joy of heart?

I only watched you landing and I know not.
But this I know, that were I in your stead,
I would not change the island that holds nothing,
For these rich mines of silver and of lead
And these pale girls whose hearts are with the dead.

XLII

MOTIFS

The tide is slack in equipoise,
Lapping the inmost reaches of the creek.
Beyond the bar's white rip the fishermen
Trim their torn sails on blocks that swell and creak
And gather in the strange cold life they seek.

Pry as a lizard, lazy on the foreshore,
I hear the harsh cicadas' monody,
And knowing there is little but this sunlight
These desultory palms, this tepid sea,
I bid Love ask no further proof of me.

In high conjunction sun and moon
Drive the spring tides across the muddy land.
The close and sentient mind is helpless here,
And I who do not fully understand,
But half forgetting, half expecting lie
And let the world fall softly from my hand,
Conceal my heart's great love and love's great fear,
And would forget you, if I could, my dear.

XLIII

BIVOUAC

There was no trace of Heaven
That night as we lay
Punch-drunk and blistered with sunlight
On the ploughed-up clay.

I remembered the cactus where our wheels
Had bruised it, bleeding white;
And a fat rat crouching beady-eyed
Caught by my light;

And the dry disturbing whispers
Of the agitated wood,
With its leathery vendetta,
Mantillas dark with blood.

And the darkness drenched with Evil
Haunting as a country song,
Ignoring the protesting cry
Of Right and of Wrong.

Yet the peasant was drawing water
With the first excited bird
And the dawn with childish eyes

Observed us as we stirred

And the milk-white oxen waited
Docile at the yoke
As we clipped on our equipment
And scarcely spoke

Being bewildered by the night
And only aware
Of the withering obsession
That lovers grow to fear
When the last note is written
And at last and alone
One of them wakes in terror
And the other is gone.

XLIV

THE JUNGLE

In mole-blue indolence the sun
Plays idly on the stagnant pool
In whose grey bed black swollen leaf
Holds Autumn rotting like an unfrocked priest.
The crocodile slides from the ochre sand
And drives the great translucent fish
Under the boughs across the running gravel.
Windfalls of brittle mast crunch as we come
To quench more than our thirst—our selves—
Beneath this bamboo bridge, this mantled pool
Where sleep exudes a sinister content
As though all strength of mind and limb must pass
And all fidelities and doubts dissolve,
The weighted world a bubble in each head,
The warm pacts of the flesh betrayed
By the nonchalance of a laugh,
The green indifference of this sleep.

II

Wandering and fortuitous the paths
We followed to this rendezvous today
Out of the mines and offices and dives,
The side streets of anxiety and want,
Huge cities known and distant as the stars,
Wheeling beyond our destiny and hope.
We did not notice how the accent changed
As shadows ride from precipice to plain

Closing the parks and cordoning the roads,
Clouding the humming cultures of the West—.
The weekly bribe we paid the man in black,
The day shift sinking from the sun,
The blinding arc of rivets blown through steel,
The patient queues, headlines and slogans flung
Across a frightened continent, the town
Sullen and out of work, the little home
Semi-detached, suburban, transient
As fever or the anger of the old,
The best ones on some specious pretext gone.

But we who dream beside this jungle pool
Prefer the instinctive rightness of the poised
Pied kingfisher deep darting for a fish
To all the banal rectitude of states,
The dew-bright diamonds on a viper's back
To the slow poison of a meaning lost
And the vituperations of the just.

III

The banyan's branching clerestories close
The noon's harsh splendour to a head of light.
The black spot in the focus grows and grows:
The vagueness of the child, the lover's deep
And inarticulate bewilderment,
The willingness to please that made a wound,
The kneeling darkness and the hungry prayer;
Cargoes of anguish in the holds of joy,
The smooth deceitful stranger in the heart,
The tangled wrack of motives drifting down
An oceanic tide of Wrong.
And though the state has enemies ,we know
The greater enmity within ourselves.

Some things we cleaned like knives in earth,
Kept from the dew and rust of Time
Instinctive truths and elemental love,
Knowing the force that brings the teal and quail
From Turkestan across the Himalayan snows
To Kashmir and the South. alone can guide
That winging wildness home again.

Oh you who want us for ourselves,
Whose love can start the snow-rush in the woods
And melt the glacier in the dark coulisse,
Forgive this strange inconstancy of soul,
The face distorted in a jungle pool
That drowns its image in a mort of leaves.

IV

Grey monkeys gibber, ignorant and wise.
We are the ghosts, and they the denizens;
We are like them anonymous, unknown,
Avoiding what is human, near,
Skirting the villages, the paddy fields
Where boys sit timelessly to scare the crows
On bamboo platforms raised above their lives.

A trackless wilderness divides
Joy from its cause, the motive from the act:
The killing arm uncurls, strokes the soft moss;
The distant world is an obituary,
We do not hear the tappings of its dread.
The act sustains; there is no consequence.
Only aloneness, swinging slowly
Down the cold orbit of an older world
Than any they predicted in the schools,
Stirs the cold forest with a starry wind,
And sudden as the flashing of a sword
The dream exalts the bowed and golden head
And time is swept with a great turbulence,
The old temptation to remould the world.

The bamboos creak like an uneasy house;
The night is shrill with crickets, cold with space.
And if the mute pads on the sand should lift
Annihilating paws and strike us down
Then would some unimportant death resound
With the imprisoned music of the soul?
And we become the world we could not change?

Or does the will's long struggle end
With the last kindness of a foe or friend?

XLV

THE ASSAULT CONVOY

Three days of waiting in the islands
Of a remote inhospitable bay
Have soured the small dry stretch of time
Which we allow to drift away
Disconsolate that death should so delay

His wild and breathless act upon the fore-shore

The seas still separate and hide.
Our hobnails stamp in crazy repetition,
Bodies' sweat to bodies' sweat confide
The intimacy we denied.

The nihilist persistence of the sun,
The engines throbbing heatedly all night,
The white refineries of salt and dust
Forbid the mind to think, the pen to write;
We trample down the fences of delight.

Perhaps the ultimate configuration
Of island and peninsula and reef
Will have the same shapes, tortuous and crannied
And the same meaning as our dark belief,
The solid contours of our native grief.

The real always fades into the meaning,
From cone to thread some grave perception drives
The twisted failures into vast fulfilments.
After the holocaust of shells and knives,
The victory, the treaty, the betrayal,
The supersession of a million lives,
The hawk sees something stir among the trenches,
The field mouse hears the sigh of what survives.

XLVI

THE RAID

The estuary silted up
The dredger rusting by the pier
The beaches red and indolent
The coolies running now with fear.

This complex expedition
Calculated, intricate,
Spills blood and pain and agony
Carefully discounting Fate.

And the needed devotion
Of terrified boys
Spread-eagles the horror
That annuls and destroys

The calm intimations,
Of lamplight on books,
The warm naked shoulder,
The harvest in stooks.

And racked with the passion
 That Life should have done,
The bleeding entrails tremble
In the merciless sun

That beats on the silted-up river,
The rusty dredger, the pier,
The indolent red beaches,
The confusion; the fear.

XLVII

A FRAGMENT

Where aloneness fiercely
Trumpets the unsounded night
And the silence surges higher
Than hands or seas or mountains' height

I the deep shaft sinking
Through the quivering Unknown
Feel your anguish beat its answer
As you grow round me, flesh and bone.

The wild beast in the cave
Is all our pride; and will not be
Again until the world's blind travail
Breaks in crimson flower from the tree

I am, in Thee.

XLVIII

MIDNIGHT IN INDIA

Here is no mined and cratered deep
As in the fenced-off landscapes of the West
Within this Eastern wilderness
The human war is lost.

The three dark quarters bow their heads
To where the fourth in radiance glows;
The withered villages look up and smile;
The moon's annunciation grows.

Oh I have set the earth aflame

And brought the high dominions down,
And soiled each simple act with shame
And had no feelings of my own.

I sank in drumming tides of grief
And in the sea-king's sandy bed
Submerged in gulfs of disbelief
Lay with the red-toothed daughters of the dead.

Until you woke me with a sigh
And eased the dark compression in my head,
And sang and did not cease when I
Broke your heart like holy bread.

We cast away the bitter death
That holds the fine circumference of life
And gathered in a single breath
All that begins and ends in man and wife

And though the painful errors grow
And youth sprawls dead beside the Gate
And lovely bodies stiffen in the snow
And old devotions breed a newer hate,

Yet time stands still upon the east
The moonlight lies in pools and human pain
Soothes the dry lips on which it lies
And I behold your calm white face again.

Mysterious tremors stir the beast,
In unknown worlds he dies;
I lie within your hands, within your peace,
And watch this last effulgent world arise.

Alun Lewis – A Concise Bibliography

Raiders' Dawn & Other Poems (1942)
The Last Inspection & Other Stories (1942)

Posthumous Releases and Compilations
Ha! Ha! Among the Trumpets. Poems in Transit (1945)
Letters from India (1946)
In the Green Tree (letters & stories) (1948)
Selected Poetry & Prose (1966)
Selected Poems of Alun Lewis (1981)
Alun Lewis. A Miscellany of His Writings (1982)
Letters to My Wife, edited by Gweno Lewis (1989)

www.ingramcontent.com/pod-product-compliance
Lightning Source LLC
Chambersburg PA
CBHW060058050426
42448CB00011B/2527